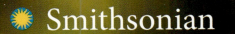
Smithsonian

LITTLE EXPLORER

SNAKES

by Martha E. H. Rustad

CAPSTONE PRESS
a capstone imprint

Little Explorer is published by Capstone Press,
1710 Roe Crest Drive, North Mankato, Minnesota 56003
www.capstonepub.com

Library of Congress Cataloging-in-Publication Data
Rustad, Martha E. H. (Martha Elizabeth Hillman), 1975– author.
Snakes / by Martha E. H. Rustad.
 pages cm. — (Smithsonian little explorer)
Summary: "Introduces types of snakes to young readers,
including diet, range, habitat, and life cycle"—Provided by
publisher.
 Audience: Grade K to 3.
 Audience: 4-8.
 Includes index.
 ISBN 978-1-4765-3935-5 (library binding)
 ISBN 978-1-4765-5183-8 (paperback)
 ISBN 978-1-4765-5271-2 (paper over board)
1. Snakes—Juvenile literature. I. Title.
QL666.O6R78 2014
 597.96—dc23   2013032351

Editorial Credits
Kristen Mohn, editor; Sarah Bennett, designer; Marcie Spence,
media researcher; Danielle Ceminsky, production specialist

Not for Andrea,
but for Eleanora and Beckett. —MEHR

Our very special thanks to Jeremy F. Jacobs, Collection Manager,
Division of Amphibians and Reptiles, National Museum of
Natural History, Smithsonian Institution, for his curatorial review.
Capstone would also like to thank Kealy Wilson, Smithsonian
Institution Project Coordinator and Product Development
Manager, and the following at Smithsonian Enterprises: Ellen
Nanney, Licensing Manager; Brigid Ferraro, Director of Licensing;
Carol LeBlanc, Senior Vice President, Consumer & Education
Products.

Image Credits
Alamy Images: AfriPics, 15 (bottom), Amazon-Images, 12-13,
blinckwinkel, 20 (top), 22 (middle), John Cancalosi, 23 (bottom),
Photoshot Holdings Ltd., 21 (bottom); Capstone Studio: Karon
Dubke, 28; Corbis: Bebeto Matthews/AP, 11 (bottom); Getty
Images: Auscape/UIG, 8 (bottom) and Leonard Lee Rue III, 23 (top
left), suebg1/Flickr, 21 (top); iStockphoto: Snowleopard1, cover;
Minden Pictures: Michael and Patricia Fogden, 15 (top), Nick
Garbutt, 11 (top); Newscom: Anthony Bannister/ZUMA Press, 25
(bottom), CB2/ZOB/WENN, 17 (bottom), Christian Hutter Image
Broker, 25 (top), Design Pics/Jody Watt, 27 (top), Mark Conlin/
ZUMA Press, 26; Shutterstock: Alberto Loyo, 12 (top), Aliaksandr
Radzko, design element, amirage, design element, Anton_Ivanov,
10 (bottom), Audrey Snider-Bell, 7 (bottom right), 22 (bottom),
AZP Worldwide, 24, Bruce MacQueen, 4, Butterfly Hunter, 9
(middle), Chantelle Bosch, 25 (middle), Coy St. Clair, 14, Curly
Pat, design element, Darren Whittingham, design element, David
Persson, 12 (bottom), DeskyCom, 2, Dr. Morley Read, 19 (bottom),
Elliotte Rusty Harold, 19 (middle), Eric Rounds, 5 (top left),
feathercollector, 15 (middle), Fotomiro, 13 (bottom), Heiko Kiera,
16, 20 (bottom), 22 (top), 29 (top and bottom left)Ivan Kuzmin,
9 (top), John A. Anderson, 27 (bottom), Ljupco Smokovski, 1
(middle), lunatic67, 7 (middle left), Matt Jeppson, 7 (top left), 8
(top), 19 (top), Matteo Photos, 7 (bottom left), mountainpix, 17
(middle), Oleg Blazhyievskyi, 10 (top), Omega77, 1 (background),
Patricia K. Campbell, 18, Paul Cowell, 7 (top right), Potapov
Alexander, design element, reptiles4all, 5 (bottom left), Ryan
M. Bolton, 5 (bottom right), 30-31, Sergey Utkin, 5 (top right),
Skynavin, 6, 17 (top), Steve Heap, 9 (bottom), stock09, design
element, Tyler Fox, 23 (top right), William Silver, 29 (bottom right),
ylq, design element

Printed in the United States of America in Stevens Point, Wisconsin.
092013   007769WZS14

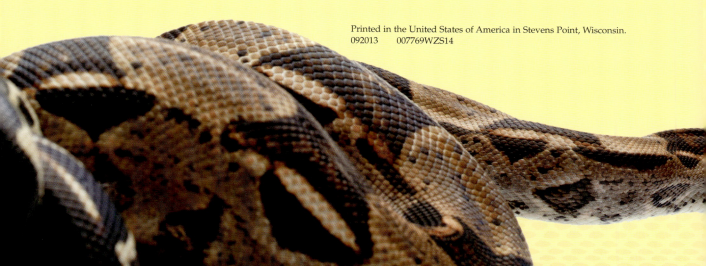

TABLE OF CONTENTS

SLITHERING SNAKES

Ssss! What's that sound? It's something slithering on the ground.

It has a long, skinny body. It has no legs. Its forked tongue darts out. It's a snake!

Snakes are reptiles. They are cold-blooded. They have scaly skin.

A snake gathers odors with its tongue. Inside its mouth is a Jacobson's organ. The snake uses this body part to taste and smell.

Snakes are predators. They hunt and eat other animals. Snakes open their jaws wide to swallow prey whole.

Jacobson's organ

SNAKE FAMILIES

There are 18 snake families. But most snakes belong to one of six families.

cobra

MAJOR SNAKE FAMILIES	
Scientific Name	Common Name
Colubridae (koh-LOO-bruh-dee)	colubrids
Boidae (BOY-dee)	boas and anacondas
Pythonidae (pie-THON-uh-dee)	pythons
Elapidae (eh-LAP-uh-dee)	cobras, mambas, and coral snakes
Viperidae (vie-PAIR-uh-dee)	vipers and rattlesnakes
Hydrophiidae (hie-druh-FIE-uh-dee)	sea snakes

colubrid

Snakes live almost everywhere in the world.

python

sea snake

viper

boa

There are about 3,000 kinds of snakes. More species are still being discovered.

COLUBRIDS

There are about 1,760 species of colubrid snakes. About two-thirds of snakes in the world are colubrids. Garter snakes and some tree snakes are colubrids.

Tree snakes live in trees. They eat frogs, birds, lizards, and other animals that live in trees. ▼

Garter snakes do not hurt people. But they sometimes poop on people who pick them up.

Garter snakes are one of the most common snakes in North America. Long stripes run along their bodies. They eat frogs, mice, worms, and bugs.

BOA CONSTRICTORS

Boa constrictors grab prey with their teeth. Then they wrap their long bodies around it and squeeze it to death. Their jaws open wide to swallow birds, monkeys, wild pigs, and other large animals.

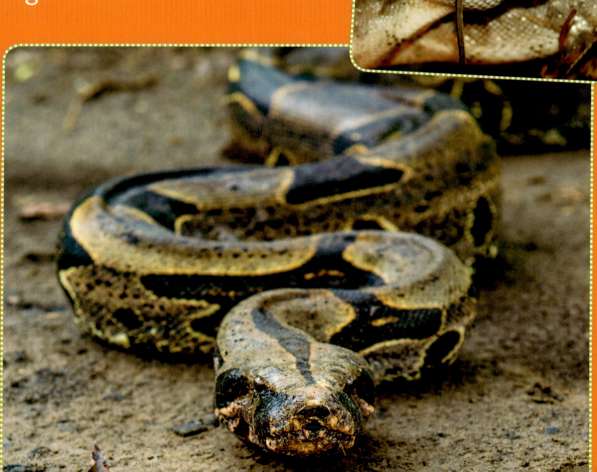

It may take six days for a boa constrictor to digest a meal.

Boa constrictors live in burrows. Their homes range from Mexico to South America.

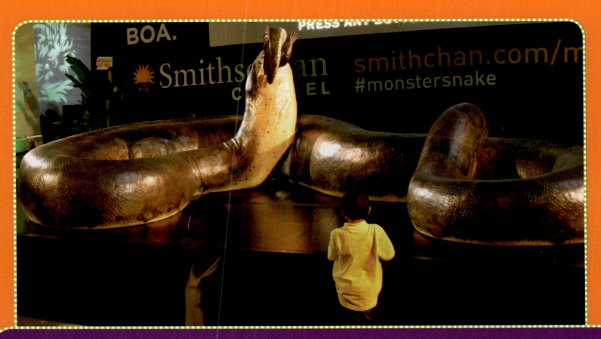

▲ Scientists found bones from Titanoboa in 2009. This extinct snake was the largest snake ever. It was 43 feet (13 meters) long and weighed more than a ton. Titanoboa lived 58 million years ago in South America.

ANACONDAS

Anacondas live in swamps and rivers in South America. They lie still underwater and surprise prey such as deer, wild pigs, and turtles.

An anaconda holds its nostrils above the water to breathe, like a crocodile.

school bus: 45 feet (13.7 m)

Green anacondas are the largest snakes in the world. They grow up to 30 feet (9.1 m) long.

human: 6 feet (1.8 m)

anaconda: 30 feet (9.1 m)

Anacondas squeeze prey until it stops breathing. Sometimes they pull prey underwater to drown it. They swallow prey whole. Months might pass before their next meal!

13

PYTHONS

Pythons smell their prey. They also sense its body heat.

They wiggle the end of their tail to trick their prey. Birds, lizards, and small mammals come near. Then pythons grab the prey.

Green tree pythons call the rain forest home.

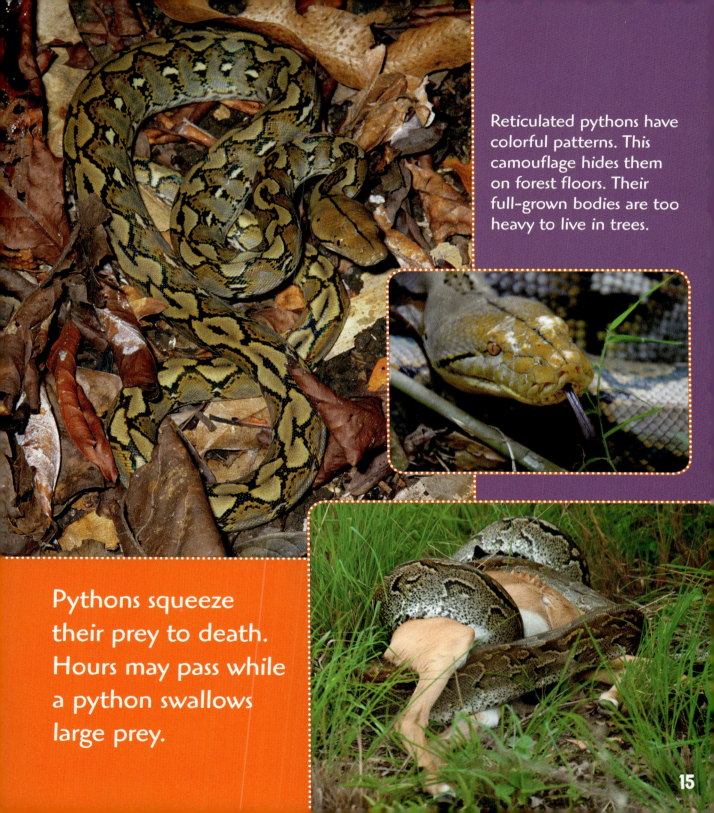

Reticulated pythons have colorful patterns. This camouflage hides them on forest floors. Their full-grown bodies are too heavy to live in trees.

Pythons squeeze their prey to death. Hours may pass while a python swallows large prey.

15

COBRAS

Cobras live in Africa and Asia. Their neck scales widen to make hoods.

They bite and kill prey with venom. Cobra venom can harm humans. A king cobra's bite is so powerful that it can kill an elephant.

Some snakes use venom to kill prey. About 300 snake species are venomous. Of those, only about 150 can kill humans. Still, each year about 20,000 people die from snakebites.

A king cobra can lift the front of its body off the ground. Its loud hiss sounds like a growl.

When scared, a spitting cobra spits venom. It aims at the predator's eyes. The venom can cause blindness.

CORAL SNAKES

Red, black, and yellow bands cover coral snakes. A bite from their short fangs kills prey quickly. They eat other snakes and lizards.

Milk snakes also have red, black, and yellow bands. But the colors are in a different order than on coral snakes. Milk snakes are harmless to humans. In North America you can remember which snake is dangerous with this rhyme:

"RED ON YELLOW, AVOID THE FELLOW:
RED ON BLACK, VENOM LACK."

Coral snakes grow as long as 5 feet (1.5 m). They live in North and South America, Africa, and Asia.

MAMBAS

Mambas live in rain forests in Africa. Their bites are deadly.

Green mambas live in trees. Their green skin helps them hide. These quick snakes slither as fast as 7 miles (11 kilometers) per hour.

A black mamba is not black. It is named for the black inside of its mouth. Its body coloring is gray or brown.

One black mamba bite has enough venom to kill as many as 40 adult humans.

Mambas, as well as most other snakes, hatch from eggs.

RATTLESNAKES

Rattlesnakes shake their tails. The sound scares some predators away.

A rattlesnake hunts at night. It strikes its prey. But its venom doesn't kill right away. The snake follows the dying prey.

Rattlesnakes are also called pit vipers. Pits between the nose and eyes feel temperature differences to find prey.

Snakes shed a layer of skin to grow. This is called molting. A rattlesnake gains another rattle each time it molts.

Rattlesnake babies are born live after hatching from eggs inside the mother's body. A female rattlesnake can have from one to 60 babies at a time!

SIDEWINDERS

Sidewinder snakes live in deserts. They move sideways. Less of their body touches the hot sand.

This helps them stay cool as they move.

Two scales grow above the eyes of the horned viper. The scales look like horns.

Sidewinders burrow under sand to stay out of the sun. It is also a good way to surprise prey. Their brown color blends in with their habitat.

SEA SNAKES

Sea snakes live in the ocean. Their tails are flat at the end like a paddle. The shape helps them swim.

Yellow-bellied sea snakes live in the Pacific Ocean. They kill fish and eels with their strong venom.

Snakes don't have ears outside their bodies.
But they still can hear some low sounds.

PET SNAKES

People keep snakes as pets.
They live inside glass cases.
People feed them dead mice and bugs.

Each year people bring thousands of pythons and boas into the United States from other countries. They sell them as pets. This is illegal in many states.

Some Burmese pythons live in south Florida. They are probably escaped pets.

Python hunters capture dangerous snakes.

Some snake species are endangered.
Too many are collected from the wild.
It isn't safe to keep wild snakes as pets.
Wild snakes live best in nature.

GLOSSARY

burrow—a hole in the ground made or used by an animal; also, to dig

cold-blooded—having a body temperature that is the same as the surroundings; all reptiles are cold-blooded

digest—to break down food so it can be used by the body

fang—a long, hollow tooth; venom flows through fangs

Jacobson's organ—an organ on the roof of the mouth of a reptile; the tongue picks up scents and carries them to the Jacobson's organ

molt—to shed an outer layer of skin

nostril—an opening of an animal's nose through which it breathes and smells

odor—a smell

predator—an animal that hunts other animals for food

prey—an animal hunted by another animal for food

range—to live within a certain area

reptile—a cold-blooded animal that breathes air and has a backbone; most reptiles lay eggs and have scaly skin

species—a group of animals with similar features

strike—attack

venom—a poison made by some snakes; snakes inject venom into prey through hollow fangs

CRITICAL THINKING USING THE COMMON CORE

Look at the graphic on page 13. Use it to compare and contrast the sizes of an anaconda, a school bus, and a person. Why do you think the author uses a graphic instead of simply listing the sizes? (Craft and Structure)

Study the information about rattlesnakes on pages 22 and 23. What did you learn about their rattles? Give details from the text. (Key Ideas and Details)

Camouflage is coloring that helps animals hide from predators or sneak up on prey. Find examples in the text of snakes that use camouflage. What other animals use camouflage? (Integration of Knolwedge and Ideas)

READ MORE

Feldman, Thea. *Snakes Up Close!* American Museum of Natural History Easy Readers. New York: Sterling Children's Books, 2012.

Higgins, Melissa. *Anacondas.* Snakes. North Mankato, Minn.: Capstone Press, 2013.

Woodward, John. *Everything You Need to Know About Snakes: And Other Scaly Reptiles.* New York: DK Pub., 2013.

INTERNET SITES

FactHound offers a safe, fun way to find Internet sites related to this book. All of the sites on FactHound have been researched by our staff.

Here's all you do:
Visit *www.facthound.com*
Type in this code: 9781476539355

Super-cool stuff! Check out projects, games and lots more at www.capstonekids.com

INDEX